WHEN LI
publishe

copyright

cover and page design by Scott Sailer

Unless otherwise indicated, Scripture quotations are from:
The Holy Bible, New International Version
Copyright 1973, 1984 by International Bible Society
Used by permission of Zondervan Publishing House

Printed in the United States of America
ALL RIGHTS RESERVED
No part of this publication may be reproduced, stored in a retrieval system, or transmitted, in any form or by any means—electronic, mechanical, photocopying, recording, or otherwise—without written permission.

For information:

Living Smart Resources
1819 Fifth Avenue
Youngstown, OH 44504
www.livingsmart.org
330-746-6626

Content categories:
Leadership
Relationship
Marriage
Religious aspects—Christianity

ISBN 0-9765513-0-6

When
LEADERS
Live Together

becoming one

when you

REALLY

are two

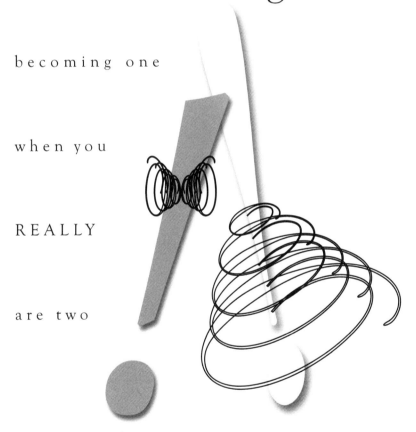

LARRY & DEVI TITUS

www.livingsmart.org

CONTENTS
when leaders live together

Introduction 3

1. HEADSHIP AND LEADERSHIP
   He says 7
   She says 13

2. DIVERSITY IS GOOD
   He says 19
   She says 27

3. RELEASER OR CONTROLLER
   He says 29
   She says 39

4. SUBMITTED AND SATISFIED
   He says 45
   She says 53

5. THE CURSE OF CRITICISM
   He says 57
   She says 71

6. ME MACHO—ME MACHOETTE
   He says 75
   She says 87

7. CAUTION ZONE—WATCH FOR RED FLAGS
   They say 93

8. LIVING WITH A LEADER
   He says 105
   She says 113

About the authors 119

INTRODUCTION

They say a book written on what?

LARRY Do you want to know why a book should be written on, *When Leaders Live Together?* It's because I needed one myself and couldn't find it. Do you know why I'm qualified to write a book on, *When Leaders Live Together?* It's because I live with a leader. No, on second thought, I live with a Leader, with a capitol "L". No, I live with a LEADER! On a scale from one to ten my wife's leadership quotient is one hundred ninety three, and climbing daily. I want you to know, "I LIVE WITH A LEADER!!!!!" Any questions?

I remember being on a 747-jet airliner one day when she tried rearranging all the seating in our section of the jumbo jet, because she wanted our family to sit together.

I remember her designing, in intricate detail, our wedding and everyone else's wedding she's attended.

I remember her witnessing a traffic accident and immediately taking over at the scene. She began helping the injured, directing traffic, calling 911, telling the policeman to turn on his blinking light, and then running down the street in hot pursuit of the hit-and-run driver. This was all done as she wore a designer suit and high heels. Nothing, and I mean nothing, is impossible for my leader/wife.

Again, are there any questions about my qualifications for writing a book on living with a leader? I live, friends, with Devi Titus, a gifted writer, magazine publisher, model, mother, conference speaker, teacher and preacher of the Word, interior designer, founder of The Mentoring Mansion, entrepreneur, and doer of anything she fixes her mind to accomplish. I think she invented the word *leader*. She was born coming out of the womb as a leader and hasn't stopped a day in her life.

Then Devi married me, a leader by obligation. I'm a leader because I'm the head of the marriage, household and thirty-four years of being a pastor. I'm a leader because I'm a man and you're supposed to be. I'm a leader because I have Biblical convictions that cause me to lead. And lastly, and most importantly, I'm a leader because my wife told me I was. So there! Amen! Any questions?

Needless to say, we've had a few disagreements in our forty-one years of marriage over *how* to lead. So that's the reason for the book. Do you, or anyone you know, relate to my situation? If so, join me

INTRODUCTION

as we discuss the rich and rewarding possibilities inherent in living with a leader.

DEVI   Well, I live with a leader too! Was there a book *When Leaders Live Together* when I needed one? No! But because Larry and I figured a few things out on our own, we think you may want to know how to manage your lives as leaders who live together.

Larry does not consider himself a leader by temperament or personality. But he has always been in positions where he is the CEO or the head of whatever he is doing. My husband has spent his career as a senior pastor, a very influential, successful pastor. In addition to leading his staff, and growing large churches, he has hundreds of men who call him "Dad". Larry's leadership is highly relational. He is people oriented. I am task oriented. Both of us are leaders, but very different.

Larry has strong opinions in some things, unusual things. He reminds me to do everything, as if I have never done it before. He is patient and kind, but has high standards. If I need to reapply my lipstick, he tells me. If my nails need to be repolished, he reminds me. However, he has no opinion on other things, important things, like investments, where to go on vacation or what to buy our children for Christmas.

Larry does not lead because it is in his personality. He leads because

INTRODUCTION

when he was a young boy, God put a mandate on his life that required leadership. He leads from convictions. He leads because of responsibility. He leads our family because he is the head of our home. He leads because I respect his position of headship, honor him, and want to follow his Godly example.

Larry does not rearrange the seating in a 747. He gives up his aisle seat and sits in the center. He does not direct traffic or tell the police officer what to do. He prays for the injured in the car. He does not spend his time working on strategies to build an organization. He spends his time building godly character in people. He does not tell a hurting pastor to read a book. He meets with him and stays in touch with him. He spends hours on the phone per day, leading people to realize their full potential.

His leadership impacts pastors, church members, neighbors, and children. I am a better person than I would have been because of Larry's leadership in my life. Larry leads with love. He lovingly sees the best in those he leads, believes in us and allows us to be better.

CHAPTER ONE

HEADSHIP AND LEADERSHIP

LARRY Did you know that there is a big difference between headship and leadership? Headship in marriage is the Biblical responsibility of the man to oversee his home and his wife, but leadership is a personality trait. If you're part of the male gender, God has called you to be the head of the marriage. The dominant leader in the home can be either the man or the woman. Not understanding this distinction has caused centuries of confusion in marriages. Men have too often tried to be a leader, because they feel obligated to be. Women have tried to subdue their leadership personality, because they feel to lead would remove them from their submissive responsibility.

I've got good news for you. If you're a man who doesn't possess leadership skills, you're not obligated to lead. However, you still must assume responsibility for headship. If you're a woman, you are free to lead according to your personality skills, as long as you don't violate the headship principle through rebellion or authoritarianism.

In case you're in doubt about the statement that the man is to be the head of the marriage, check out these scriptures:

Now I want you to realize that the head of every man is Christ, and the head of the woman is man, and the head of Christ is God. I Corinthians 11:3

For the husband is the head of the wife as Christ is the head of the church, his body, of which he is the Savior. Ephesians 5:22

In understanding headship, you must realize that man is the one who is ultimately responsible before God for the marriage. It's a gender thing. It doesn't relate to a man's qualifications, abilities, or personality. It relates to only one thing, that God, in his divine prerogative as creator, has called man, not woman, to be the head. If women have a problem with that, I suggest they take it up with God. It was His decision.

Leadership, on the other hand, is a personality trait. The dominant leadership personality in the home could be either the man or the woman, or a combination of both. As I described in the Introduction, my wife came out of the womb being a leader. She was a leader at school, around her friends, at home, and, guess what, she's a leader in our marriage. She's a natural leader. From the time her feet hit the floor in the morning, until she goes to bed at night, she leads.

It's a personality thing. Yet she has willingly chosen to honor and submit to my headship in our marriage and home under Christ.

Because Devi is a leader, that leaves but two options for me. I can either suppress her or release her. Many men married to gifted leaders, out of insecurity or not understanding the marriage roles, have tried to suppress and control their wives. They don't let their leadership skills be released. They refuse to give them a voice in the marriage. They don't allow them to express themselves. What a shame! Often the wife will have superior leadership skills that would serve the husband well in his own growth, if only he would allow her the freedom to express her gifts.

Unfortunately, even if you try to suppress your wife's personality it won't work. She can cover it, mask it, and submit to you, but she can never change who she is, no more than you can change your personality. Furthermore, God doesn't want her to. He wants her to be herself—who He created her to be. He wants the man to appreciate her leadership gifts and release them.

Our friends, Richmond and Anna McCoy, who are both strong leaders, have a great concept, called the "increase, decrease" principle. Taking their cues from John the Baptist, who had to decrease so that Jesus could increase, they choose to honor each other by knowing when it's time to decrease so that their partner can increase. It's a decision that should come quite naturally when two people are committed to each other in love. No special manuals or directions should be required. You should know instinctively when circumstances arise that this is either the time for me to increase and her to decrease, or for me to decrease so that she can increase.

Paul says in Philippians 2:3 that we are to *do nothing out of selfish ambition or vain conceit, but in humility consider others better than ourselves.* In a similar vein he says in Ephesians 4:2,3, to be, *completely humble and gentle; be patient, bearing with one another in love. Make every effort to keep the unity of the Spirit through the bond of peace.*

For clarity let's give some illustrations of the difference between headship and leadership in marriage:

Headship is oversight of the entire home and marriage.

Headship is the sole responsibility of the man.

Headship provides the covering for the wife's leadership skills.

Headship requires that the man understand that he himself is under the headship of Christ.

Headship understands that the buck stops with him.

Headship is to be patterned after the headship of Christ.

Headship is the final arbiter in deciding direction in the home.

Headship is the final point of authority in the home.

On the other hand,

Leadership can be a combination of skills, from either the wife or the husband.

Leadership can be predominant in one of the spouses.

Leadership is closely connected to abilities and personality.

Leadership is a natural gift to influence people.

Leadership must be recognized and released by the head of the home to be effective.

Leadership can be shared by both spouses.

Depending on their maturity, leadership responsibilities can be recognized and released in children as well.

The most important question for you, sir, is are there any areas in which your wife is gifted but you have refused to allow her the freedom to exercise her leadership? It would be good for both of you if you could confess the areas in which you have suppressed her leadership so that she could be fully released to fulfill her calling in God.

The greatest joy for me, as a husband, is to see my wife released and fully functioning in her gifts, personality and calling. If that requires that I decrease in some areas, so that she might increase, so be it. I am the only one who can give my wife wings to soar.

CHAPTER ONE

HEADSHIP AND LEADERSHIP

DEVI Larry has addressed headship and leadership from a male perspective in marriage. I want to elaborate more on this topic from a practical perspective that is a bit broader in scope.

It is my conviction that the misunderstanding of these roles has caused great confusion in organizations, churches, and especially families. I am not addressing this topic to defend myself as a leader, nor to discredit the importance of submission, both in marriage and in corporate relationships. I fully understand that the principle of authority and functioning with right relationships to authority is vital to good character. Proper submission to authority is releasing in anyone's life.

Larry made it very clear that headship and leadership are not synonyms. Neither are they gender assigned, except in marriage. Too often the terms headship and leadership are used interchangeably.

When this is done it confuses the roles and responses of those involved.

I want to elaborate a bit more on the difference between headship and leadership:

Headship is assigned authority. Headship holds the top position of leadership. However, there can be several tiers of leadership under headship. It is also possible for the head to not be a good leader. Headship unlike leadership has one tier. Following is a quick overview of the attributes of headship:

1. Heads are the authority.
2. Heads oversee.
3. Heads release leaders to work under them.
4. Heads should be team builders.
5. Heads can be male or female except in marriage according to Biblical standards.
6. Headship has boundaries.

Let me illustrate headship with this scenario:

If you are stopped by a Highway Patrolman and are cited for driving too fast, you must submit to him or her. If you don't, you will be penalized. Why? Because they have assigned authority that is backed by our law. The fact that they are now in headship over you does not mean they are leading you, nor does it prove that they are a good leader.

Now, you may be a very influential leader commanding the respect of thousands in your company. Perhaps you are even the head—the CEO. However, as soon as those blinking lights were turned on, your role changed in this situation. When the patrolman stops you, who is the head and who is the leader? The patrolman is the head and you remain a leader, but not his leader.

Do you say to him, "Officer, I am a great leader and you are not, so I do not have to pay this ticket," or do you say, "Well, I'll pay the ticket if you will begin leading." No! You submit to his headship and do what he says. You drive to your place of employment and continue leading. When you go home, if you are the husband, you now offer oversight to your family and your wife, releasing their leadership under your authority.

Unfortunately, when a leader wife is married to a non-leader husband, too often she attempts to coerce him into doing what is not natural to him. Because he is the head of the wife, and has assigned Biblical responsibility to her, he should oversee her with sensitivity and release her to serve their family with her leadership skills.

Leadership unlike headship has multiple facets:

1. Leadership has various styles.
2. Leadership can be learned.

3. Leadership is natural to some and unnatural to others depending on their personality.

4. Leaders have followers.

5. Leaders are influential.

6. Leaders instruct.

7. Leaders delegate.

8. Leaders respect those they influence.

Wives who are natural leaders must be careful to not instruct their husbands, always teaching them and telling them what to do. If a wife has headship authority and leadership responsibility at her place of employment, she should be very aware to remove her "boss" hat as she is driving into her driveway and enter her home with a servant's attitude. Your leadership skills should be used to train your children in responsibility, but cannot be directed toward your husband. As you submit to his headship and honor him as the head of your family, you will have peace in your home and in your relationship.

I am a woman and I am a natural leader. My mother tells a story of when I was in kindergarten. I began completely organizing my kindergarten class into lines. At my command one line went to the swings, another line went to the teeter-totters and another went to the monkey bars. At my command again, each group changed positions. The amazing thing is that the kids really did what I told them to do! Remember, leaders have followers—I had followers at the age of five.

Who created me to be this way? God did. Did he know that I was a woman? Of course! So is it OK for me to lead? Yes! However, because I am a woman and understand headship, it is very necessary for me to honor and respect men, even if I have authority over them. No leader, whether male or female, should relate to another person in a condescending manner. Good manners and kindness should always prevail.

Men who are submitted to the headship of a woman, and are learning from her leadership, should likewise treat her like a lady, not like another one of the guys. In a professional setting, men should still give up his seat to her, rise when she enters a room or approaches a table, and assist her with your masculine strength considering her as the weaker, not the dumber, vessel. In the same way, women who have authority should relate to men with good manners, gracious conduct, and feminine softness. Remember, you only have to try to prove who you are not. You never have to prove who you are.

Whether a head or a leader, it is important to consider the other person more important than yourself. In this way, when leaders live together, you will double your blessings.

CHAPTER TWO
He says  / go north when she goes south

DIVERSITY IS GOOD

LARRY Ever since God performed the first surgery in the Garden of Eden, that removed Eve from the side of Adam, men have been complaining that women are so different. Duh! Obviously! That's the whole purpose for God removing the side of Adam and making Eve out of it. God wanted Eve to be part of Adam, but totally different from him. Men, your rib is no longer in your side, but is sitting across the table looking at you. She sees things differently than you. She hears things differently than you. She responds differently than you. She cries at the drop of a hat. And, praise God, she looks differently than you. And what is it that you're complaining about?

I learned about diversity around forty-one years ago when on our honeymoon I first tried to find a parking space. My bride of one day instantly spotted a parking space in a different location than I, with my ultimate reasoning, had already decided upon. Since then there has not been a single day go by that I haven't zigged when she zagged. Things that are totally logical to me are completely illogical to her, and vice-versa. I go north when she goes south. I turn left when she turns right. We will even respond to people's questions with her saying, "Yes," while I am simultaneously saying, "No." To the very same question, mind you! I stand in amazement at how different we are. How could one so beautiful be wrong so often? I've questioned God's wisdom in creating women on several occasions.

Notice that God didn't create two people. He only created one. He just made two persons out of the one creation. So in reality, everything that the man does or says is only half the answer. The other half of the answer lies with the person who is the other half of him.

God's grand design is that two totally different people would come together in the covenant of marriage and unite together as one. It takes the two opposite opinions and viewpoints to come to the best decision.

Isn't it interesting that before a couple is married they are attracted to each other because of their differences? Then as soon as they say, "I do," what used to be cute is now annoying. What used to be a truism, "Opposites attract," after marriage becomes, "Opposites repel."

There is another thing that needs to be addressed. God has not called us to change the personality of our spouse. After marriage we often feel that God has gifted us with the gift of "criticism," so we can actively change the things we don't like about our partner. Well, I've got news for you. He hasn't. God wants you to appreciate your differences in style and personality, not attempt to conform them to your own image. God created us in his image, then put us together and said, "Learn to work together. Each of you has the perfect ingredient to compliment the other."

One of the most powerful scriptures in the entire Word of God is found in Matthew 18:19: *Again, I tell you that if two of you on earth agree about anything you ask for, it will be done for you by my Father in heaven.*

The word, "agree," comes from the same Greek word that we get our English word, "symphony" from. Jesus says that if two people will begin to harmonize, God will do anything for you that you ask of him. God always listens to the sounds of harmony. He's not looking for solos, either by the man or the woman. Whether its voices or instruments, music sounds better when diverse tones are interjected. Even solos are dead, hollow and unappealing without background music. Too often marriages are the result of one of the spouses working totally by themselves without the compliment of the other's contribution.

Even God works in harmony and symphony with the Son and Holy Spirit. Nothing is done without the cooperation of the other. Then he set the entire universe to work in symphony as well. If the universe was created to work in tandem, how much more so was mankind, the crowning point of his creation? Marriage partners must learn to harmonize. Remember, God is listening. Until He hears a symphony, He is under no obligation to answer your prayers.

God created the entire universe, from the heavens to the animals, by his voice. "And God said," was all that was needed to bring something out of nothing.

God did more than just "speak" man into existence, however, he came to earth and personally formed him out of the dust of the ground. Man is God's creative energy at its best, because he not only created man, but he created man in his own image. Following that, he took the woman out of the man. Then he brought the two back together and told them to become one. Biblical unity is not "oneness," its harmony. It's two people bringing their differing talents, opinions and insights together for the common good. Remember, unity is not an option; it is a command of God.

In God's divine economy and wisdom, he chose to bring opposites together so that in their choice to unify they would have a more complete picture and could accomplish more. You should be praising

God that you are opposites. If you had not come from different backgrounds and personalities, your decisions would have no balance, safety, wisdom or success. It's your diversity that allows for effectiveness.

This would be a good time to stop and reflect, maybe even write down, the areas in which you and your spouse are different. Then after you have listed them, take time to praise God for the differences:

For instance, in a man's case he might say of his wife:

She's emotional and I'm rational.

She's practical and I'm visionary.

She's multi-tasked and I'm single-tasked.

She's outgoing and I'm introverted.

She's quiet and I'm extroverted.

She's socially needy and I have few social needs.

A woman might say:

He's content to stay at home, while I want to socialize.

He's prone to make snap decisions when purchasing things, while I want to take time to compare prices and think it through.

He's content to watch television, when I want to do projects.

He's quick to offer solutions, when I want to talk about the problem.

He's suspicious of people, while I'm more trusting of them.

He's slow at reaching conclusions, while I can process them immediately.

I think it's time to verbally praise God for your differences. When the two of you work to compliment, rather than oppose, each other, what you have viewed as obstacles, you will find to be assets. It is only when you bring the two viewpoints, insights, opinions and observations together, will you become valuable to each other and the kingdom of God. Most importantly, what each of you is lacking, the other one most likely possesses. Doesn't that seem logical? If God removed that part of your personality at creation, it is only restored through marriage. No longer view each other's differing viewpoints as negative. They are extremely positive and necessary for the success of both of you.

I often hear couples say, "I can't let her (or him) know she's right or she'll think she won." Won what? Is this a battle? Do you think your spouse is your enemy? You're not fighting on opposite sides. This is not a war. You're on the same side. Any victory for hers is a victory for you. Who cares who is right when the rightness of one automatically makes it right for the other?

Marriage is an exact replication of the Body of Christ, many members operating under one head, for the purpose of accomplishing God's purpose on earth. Diversity is as important in the marriage as it is in the Body of Christ. Learn to appreciate your differences rather than despise them. Start making a symphony. Two are much better than one, when they learn to harmonize.

CHAPTER TWO
She says *Let diversity become your strength*

DIVERSITY IS GOOD

DEVI Larry zigs and I zag, so he says. Don't confuse this with Larry thinks he is right and I think he is wrong. Zigging and zagging has nothing to do with right or wrong. When I sew and set the zig-zag stitch on the machine, I do this for one reason—to prevent the seam from unraveling. The harmonizing of our diverse viewpoints strengthens our decisions. It enlarges our personal perspectives and unifies our ultimate direction.

Larry says that when my feet hit the floor in the morning the first sounds he hears are pitter-patters, in a fast pace. He thinks I have only one pace—fast. Together, we are the typical example of the tortoise and the hare. While the hare runs fast, gets tired and sleeps beside the road, the slow tortoise paces himself and wins the race.

Larry is right! Diversity is good! I don't even like being with people who are just like me. They exhaust me. I know what they are going to say, before they say it. Now, Larry, after forty one years, still keeps me guessing. I have never figured him out, and I hope I never do. He and others similar to him stimulate me.

I love listening to him. I always want to know what he thinks. In fact, it fascinates me to understand that he "thinks" before he speaks. Me? I speak and then think about what I just said. Sometimes I don't even believe what I said, after I have really thought about it.

I love the silent times we spend together, in the same room, saying nothing. At least, he says nothing and I usually break the silence. He smiles at me with adoring eyes.

Please don't try to change your spouse into your image. If you do, you will not like him or yourself. Your solo song will be sung flat rather than a duet sung in beautiful harmony. You need him and he needs you.

CHAPTER THREE
He says
Become a husband releaser

RELEASER OR CONTROLLER

LARRY For the sake of simplicity I'll put all men in the category of either "Releasers" or "Controllers." Obviously that is much too general and simplistic, but it will work for now.

Controllers are those hearty, heady, heavy-handed, half-witted, hare-brained, hard-mouthed, hard-nosed, hapless, hopeless, hoggish, hairless hominids, with less guts than a halophile (a salty ocean organism. It doesn't really fit, but I needed another "h" word) who feel that the only way they can maintain their dominance is to control and suppress their wives. These are men I will not be sending Christmas cards to this year, because I feel they are absolutely dangerous. How dare they take the beautiful gift that God has given them and keep her suppressed for the sake of inflating their own egos and stroking their false machismo. That form of masculine pride needs to be flushed down the porcelain facility. It is not Biblical.

Controllers lead with anger, intimidation, manipulation, suppression and force. They lead, all right, but it's all negative and destructive. People follow them, not out of respect, but fear. They turn their beautiful wives into cringing, fawning, cowering, fearful objects of darkness—slaves to a beastly husband. Through the years you'll notice their wife's light-filled countenance slowly become sullen, silenced, drawn, and darkened, until they give up hope and the light of their personality eventually dims and goes out completely. I would not want to be in that man's shoes on judgment day, when he will have to give account to God for abusing his authority.

I've seen once beautiful women become hardly recognizable because of insecure, heavy-handed husbands. If you're one of these men, you need to repent to your wife, to Jesus, to your children, to your employees and anyone else you've manhandled. You might need to take your repentance all the way to the President in the Oval Office, just to make sure it's cleaned out of your system. If people are following you for any other reason than the good, godly example you have set for them, then you're out of sync with the Holy Spirit and the entire Word of God. Your goal should be that people **want**, not **have**, to follow you.

Submission should always be subjective, because the wife understands the Biblical principles that are a necessary part of all leadership. Not because she's forced to be submitted by the heavy-handed personality of the husband. Obedience should never be coerced or cajoled. If the wife is forced to submit, it's not by her volition and it violates the entire Word of God.

Much of what is viewed as rebellion in a woman is nothing more than resistance against being controlled and manipulated by an insecure man, who is afraid of what she might become if he loses control.

Conversely, outbursts of anger in a controlling husband are caused not by past hurts, but by the frustration that comes when people, especially his wife, don't conform to his controlling agenda. It makes him mad when things and people don't line up to his demands. In an insecure man's army he is the general and everyone else, especially his wife, are the privates.

This again is simplistic, but I believe that a control issue is a pride issue--male pride in its most deadly form. Though he's an adult he's still playing the childhood game of "King of the Mountain." He's King and he owns the mountain.

Men, your calling is not to control your wife, but to release her. Release her to become all God created her to be. Don't be afraid that she will become better than you. Praise God if she does. Don't be afraid that she will gain more attention or notoriety than you. Praise

God if she does. Don't be afraid that she will make more money than you. Praise God for the blessing.

It is impossible for your wife to excel without it bringing honor to you. She is a reflection of you. If she shines, it's because she's catching the glow from you. I Corinthians 11:7 states that the woman is the glory of the man. If you're radiant, she'll be radiant. If you are clouded by your distorted, controlling spirit, she cannot properly reflect you without uncovering your darkness. When you shine, it will immediately be seen in her countenance. If you want to know what the husband looks like, look in the mirror of his wife's face. That will tell you volumes.

The opposite of the **controlling** husband is the **releasing** husband. You can't have it both ways. You're either a controller or a releaser. So the first question is obviously, which one are you? If I've described you in the first several paragraphs, then it's time to change. Do you want to be like Christ?

Jesus took 12 common men, and except for Judas, made everyone of them uncommon. The uneducated followers of Christ turned the world upside down, or maybe I should say, right side up. The way He brought these failed fisherman and their cohorts into release is the same way you can bring release to your wife.

He believed in them. They knew that Jesus was for them. There was no doubt. They would follow their Lord to the ends of the earth, and they did, because of his commitment to them. It's true that believing in someone is an expression of love, but it's more than that. It's letting them know in no uncertain terms that you are for them, that you're with them, that you're behind them, and that you're committed to their success.

He gave them his authority. Every time Jesus sent the disciples out with the Kingdom message, he gave them the authority to replicate what they had seen him do. One of the fears that men have is that their wife might excel their own successes. Jesus was evidently not afraid of that possibility. In John 14:12-14 he promised that his disciples would do even greater works than he had accomplished. He wasn't afraid of being upstaged by their success. His final words to them in Matthew 28:18,19 indicated that they were to be possessors of the same authority that the Father had given Him.

He allowed them to fail in His presence without berating them. Not one of the disciples made it through the three and a half years of training without having notable failures. Of course Peter comes immediately to mind, but he was not alone. On the final night in the Garden, as well as their courtyard encounter in the palace of Caiaphas, they all forsook Jesus and fled. Not one remained loyal. Yet the scripture never records Jesus berating, scolding, or humiliating them. In fact, he hosted them for a home-cooked breakfast on the shores of Galilee in the days following their defeat. He honored them when they were at their lowest so they could be released to their highest potential.

He loved them with unqualified love. God's love is always unqualified. You don't have to earn it. A person cannot be truly secure unless they have an environment of unqualified love in which to live and excel. If you want your spouse to be secure, released, fulfilled and joyful, give her unqualified love. Love her, says Paul in Ephesians 5:25, the way that Christ loved the church; a love that took him to the cross; a love that willingly laid down his life for her so that she might live.

He left His glory with them when he returned to the Father. A releasing husband makes plans for the future of his wife after he has died. He wants her to be cared for, blessed, comfortable and enjoying the fruits of their labor together even after he is no longer there to care for her himself. Jesus' final prayer was that the Father would give to the disciples the same glory that he had with the Father before the creation of the world. Every blessing that God has given you must be passed on to your wife and posterity. Don't stop the glory. Don't stop the blessing. Don't begrudge your wife what is rightfully hers. Leave your wife an inheritance that shows you cared enough for her to ensure her security after your death.

He prayed for them. Prayer can never be substituted by any other activity. The final prayer of Jesus was for His disciples. He desired that they have His glory, his unity and his Father's protection. Prayer for your wife deposits a blessing into her life that is irreplaceable and non-reproducible. Because you are Biblically the head of your wife, when you pray for her it provides an impenetrable shield of faith that provides for her protection, blessing, anointing and release. The greatest gift you can ever give your wife is your devoted, daily prayer on her behalf.

He saw potential in them. He saw them for what they would become, not what they were. He changed Simon's name to Peter, knowing that someday Peter would become a rock. As one person said, in the presence of sinners He dreamed of saints. He concentrated not on their weaknesses, but on their strengths. He had faith that they would fulfill their greatest potential. He saw the finished vessel when it was still a lump of clay. He encouraged them to go for it. "You can do it!" A "releaser" husband will give the confidence to his wife that she can do anything.

He led them by example. Leadership by coercion and intimidation was not Jesus' style. They saw him pray. They witnessed his miracles. They saw him love the unlovely. They saw Christ live a life of purity, sincerity and truth. He was touchable, compassionate and warm, not distant or aloof. He loved children and taught them to love children. He loved sinners and encouraged them to do the same. He was meek, but not soft. He had authority, but never abused it. He earned, not demanded, respect. He relied totally on the Father for direction. He put the Father's will foremost and sought only to do those things that brought glory to the Father. He was driven not by the people's needs, but by what the Father determined. Most of all he was completely obedient to the will of the Father.

He served them. Putting on the garments of a servant and washing the disciples feet at the last supper wasn't intended to impress them. It wasn't a theatrical stunt. It was who he was. True leadership, Jesus' style, is always to serve your way into it. Promotion in Christ, comes not from getting up, but from kneeling down. Serving should not be the "love language" of a few men who know no other way in which to express their love, but an active part of every man's life. When you arrive home from work at night, don yourself with your serving clothes. It's time to serve, not recline in front of the television with your wife and children catering to your whims and the dog delivering your paper. You serve them first, and then they can reverse the process.

He gave them gifts. In addition to breathing on the disciples in the Upper Room on resurrection night, Jesus also poured out the Father's promise of the Holy Spirit on the Day of Pentecost. Jesus had hardly departed into the heavens and seated Himself at the Father's right hand, when the gifts began to arrive. Men quite often fail to understand a woman's need for gifts. Unless she drops a multitude of hints prior to a birthday or anniversary, the possibility remains that the special day will slip away without receiving any token of his affection. Where are the gifts men? It's less important what they are than that THEY ARE! To a woman gifts mean sensitivity, love and thoughtfulness. Because all *good and perfect gifts* come from the Father, you become an extension of the Father's beneficence when you give.

He was a GENTLE man. He knew how to treat women. He was humble and meek in His spirit. Matthew 12 says that he never argued, raised the volume of his voice in the streets, and was so gentle that he refused to break a bent reed or to snuff out a smoking wick. He was a GENTLE man. That's the derivation of the word, "gentleman." To be a "gentleman", men, you must be a GENTLE man. A REAL man is not braggadocios, bombastic, loud, insensitive, or full of arrogant bravado. He is gentle. He leads with gentleness, not force. He doesn't need volume or anger to enforce his leadership. He's not afraid that his sensitivity will be misconstrued as weakness, because he's secure in whom he is in Jesus.

Men, you're either a Controller or a Releaser. Make your decision today. Who have you been in the past, and who do you want to be in the future? As soon as God sees your heart, witnesses your desire to change, he will help you do the rest. Let's get started! I'm behind you!

CHAPTER THREE

She says release your partner with Praise

RELEASER OR CONTROLLER

DEVI Larry writes to men almost as if women do not need to take inventory. But I want to ask the wife, "Are you a controller or a releaser?" Do you need to direct, dictate, dominate, disagree, disarm, and disengage the decisions or should I say, the attempted decisions of your husband?

When he has a suggestion about simple things: where to eat, what to wear, or what to do, do you usually make an alternate suggestion? Do you subtly think your ideas are better than his?

The results of the feminist philosophy in the way women think about men have not given us the freedom and fulfillment that they promised. Rather, this independent, self-indulgent way of thinking has led us to habits that destroy the very character of healthy, gratifying relationships. We are taught to think, "If I don't take care of myself, who will?" In terms of assuming personal responsibility this is true.

However this attitude is one that goes way beyond personal responsibility. It is an attitude of self protection, self exaltation, self gratification and self centered living.

The equal rights motivation behind feminism has now escalated to women wanting to dominate men—to be equal doesn't seem to be enough. Early in the movement, feminist leaders sponsored campaigns insisting that women no longer be portrayed in sexual roles. They were very vocal, seeking to change the public image of women. Their goal was to influence the media to redress women in "Power" suits.

Recently, while I was traveling, a young professional woman sat beside me on the airplane. She began leafing through the pages of the several magazines that she had brought on board. I could tell this was not recreational reading but her profession was related to something on these magazine pages.

She hesitated at an advertisement and studied it carefully. The captivating model on the page was scantily dressed and seductively posed. I intruded on her deep thought with this question: "Where are our feminist leaders now? Earlier in the movement they spoke against women being used in this way, insisting that our public image be one of professionalism and power." I was horrified by her response. She deliberately looked and me, pressed her index finger onto the page and said, "This is power."

I was speechless. I had nothing more to say. My mind raced remembering stories of women sitting in my office, devastated because their husbands' were addicted to pornography. She was right. Feminists no longer lobby for the professional image of women; they are content to control men regardless of how it is done. Advertisers know this and use the power of women to ensnare men.

Women's magazines now bare titles such as SELF, and ME. These titles enforce the "me-first" mentality. Such attitudes put others in second positions. This way of thinking keeps us from "considering others more important than ourselves." It is impossible to release your spouse unless you are willing to let them be first. I'm amazed how effective the simple "golden rule" is in relationships. "Do for others what you want them to do for you." It really works!

Women usually control by manipulation and seduction. We are champions at maneuvering circumstances, situations, and conversations in such a way that we can determine our preferred outcome. We barter and seduce, "If you do this, I'll do that." Unless women become aware of their powerful but sometimes subtle force they will slowly take control without knowing that they are controlling.

Controlling does not make you happy. In fact, after you have successfully taken control and your husband allows you to make all decisions, soon you will feel exhausted, emotionally tired, and internally resentful that he is not leading. If this is the case and you want to turn things around, where do you begin? You may ask, "How do I become a releaser rather than a controller?"

Change your MIND. Change the way you think. Think on the positive. *"Whatever is true, honorable, right, pure, lovely, of good report, if there is any excellence, and if anything worthy of praise, let your mind dwell (fix your mind) on these things."* Philippians 4:8

Make a list of your husband's positive attributes. Even though the lawn looks like a cow pasture before he mows it, rather than harping on this, think of other things that he does really well. Write them down to remind yourself and to place these things first in your mind.

Your thoughts become words—your words become actions—your actions become habits—your habits become your character. WOW! It's no wonder that the wisdom of scripture tells us to fix our minds on the best attributes of others.

Release your partner with praise. Speak words of affirmation, confidence, hope, and possibility to your husband. Believe in him. Learn about the things he likes and participate in things that are important to him. Do not belittle him.

You have the power to make him a king and to be his crown or to decay his character by shaming him. Proverbs 12:4 says it this way. *"An excellent wife is the crown of her husband but she who shames him is as rottenness in his bones."*

Take action. Physically affirm him. If he is balding, talk about how handsome you think bald men are. If he lacks muscle, tell him how much you like slim trim men.

Create a new habit of connecting. Kiss and hug him at least 10 times per day. When you enter and exit his presence, speak to him. Wink at him from across a room.

Larry and I can be on opposite sides of a large auditorium. Perhaps he is approaching the platform to speak. He will look for me and allow his eyes to meet mine. I smile. My smile says, "I believe in you. I'm praying for you. I'm proud to be your wife."

Not long ago, Larry was a guest speaker on Father's Day at a very large church in Southern California. I was the Sunday evening speaker on the same day. When I approached the platform, I glanced at him. He winked. That was all I needed. His wink affirmed me, supported me, believed in me, and released me to be my best for that congregation.

Supportive thoughts, words, actions and habits create the

foundation of character that, relationally, stands the test of time. You will notice your husband's weaknesses becoming stronger and you will be less bothered by them.

There is an age old saying, "Behind every good man is a woman." This saying had to come from somewhere. Most women do not realize or take responsibility for the power that they have over men. Likewise, selfish, controlling women are usually the ones behind men who fail. Their mothers or wives did not believe in them, touch them or love them.

Fear often prohibits women from releasing their husband. The truth is, you cannot control and release at the same time. So what do you fear? Security? You think if you trust your husband, he will not do what will be best for you and for your family? You are not willing to risk?

Well, I'm here to tell you that releasing your partner puts you at risk. But that's OK. His failure may bring you pain. However his success brings you prosperity. Release him to take risks and be willing to share in the outcome. All success requires elements of risk. Your refusal to allow him to venture and conquer will kill his initiative and deprive you from sharing in his joy and fulfillment.

Fear not! Turn loose. Reposition yourself and enjoy the blessings of seeing your husband prosper.

CHAPTER FOUR

SUBMITTED AND SATISFIED

LARRY The subject of submission is generally taught to women. There's a reason for that, and it's not because women are more rebellious. The reason is most sermons on submission are taught by men. Therefore it becomes logical that men would want to distract attention from them, right? What male preacher would willingly incriminate himself? The answer is, not many. For the purpose of addressing the unaddressed, I will address this address to the male addressees only. So women, sit back, enjoy, gloat if need be, give a high five to someone nearby, but no elbowing please.

A joke made the rounds of the church circuit several years ago about the man who had heard for the first time a teaching on submission and how his wife should immediately submit to his authority. He was delighted that he could go home, instruct his wife in this newfound doctrine, and set his marriage in order. After he delivered his jeremiad to his wife, he didn't see her for a while. Then after about two weeks he began to see her out of one eye. I'm sure, all the women said, "Amen!" and the men said, "Oh, me."

The Bible's teaching on submission, unlike most teaching coming from pulpits over the past three decades, is a principle that relates to both men and women, not just women. Authority, wrongfully used, can be devastating.

Authority that is exercised properly is a liberating, productive, successful, and a highly effective organizational model. Conversely, authority that is heavy-handed, unilateral, suppressive and dictatorial is evil, non-Biblical, ungodly and devastating. Furthermore, the misuse of authority, as demonstrated by dictators for centuries, can become demonic.

Please note, what distinguishes Satan's authority from that of the Holy Spirit, is his hatred of submission. Satan demands authority from his subjects but resists submission to other authorities, especially that of Jesus Christ.

The devil knows that Biblical authority would require that he himself would also have to submit to the lordship of Christ. No wonder he has stirred up such resistance and opposition to the submission teaching. Satan hates the doctrine of submission. Submission is what keeps authority from becoming evil. The devil craves authority but not submission. Maybe someone should tell Satan and his crowd that they will submit either in this life or the next, but they will submit. They have no choice. For eventually, *every knee will bow and every tongue will confess that Jesus Christ is Lord.* Philippians 2:10,11

Do you see how important it is for all who exercise authority to be under authority? Jesus had authority because he was submitted to the authority of the Father. You will have authority because you're submitted to Jesus and others who are above you. Your wife and children will have authority as they submit to your authority.

It is dangerous for a leader to exercise authority without being submitted to headship himself. The harness of submission is beneficial. It is what creates the brokenness, humility and compassion that produce a good leader. But more importantly, if a leader doesn't maintain submission to a still higher authority, he risks abusing his own authority as well as losing his authority.

Submission is essential for effective headship. A submitted heart is a surrendered heart to obedience. Submission that comes from a begrudging subservient attitude to leadership undermines the effectiveness of submission. This kind of attitude will destroy the leader's success. "Oh, I guess I'll submit if I have to," doesn't cut the mustard with your authority nor does it move the hand of God. God knows your heart and man suspects your motives.

Godly authority, exercised under Biblical guidelines, with the leader being fully submitted to those above him, should be the ultimate goal of all leaders. Leadership that is not submitted to other leaders in time will eventually fail.

Submission is God's idea. The word for submission is a military term meaning to put yourself under one who has a higher position than you. The Greek word, "hupotasso" comes from the word, "hupo", a preposition meaning "under", and "tasso," a verb meaning to "arrange in an orderly fashion."

Everyone in God's army must be lined up under someone. If you're a lieutenant you will be under a captain. If you're a captain you will be under a major. If you're a major you'll be under a colonel. If you're a colonel you'll be under a general. And if you're a private you will be under everyone. And we all start out in God's army as privates. But all must be lined up before God will honor your authority. God does not move corporately or individually until everyone has fallen in line and is functioning in their prescribed position.

In the scripture submission is not a gender issue. Everyone must be "under" authority or they are not qualified to be "over" anyone. It's a simple rule. Memorize it. You can't be **over** until you're **under.**

- Jesus was submitted to his parents. Luke 2:51
- Demons were submitted to the disciples. Luke 10:17,20
- Israel sinned by not submitting to the righteousness of God. Romans 10:3

- Believers are to be submitted to all forms of authority. Romans 13:1

- The spirits of the prophets are to be submitted to the prophets. I Corinthians 14:32

- Believers are to be submitted to each other. Ephesians 5:21

- Wives are to be submitted to their husbands. Ephesians 5:22; Colossians 3:18; Titus 2

- The Church is to be submitted to Christ. Ephesians 5:25

- Servants are to be submitted to their masters. (Employees to Employers) Titus 2:9

- The whole world is to be submitted to Christ. Hebrews 2:5

- Everyone is to be submitted to the Father of spirits. Hebrews 12:9

- Believers are to be submitted to God before resisting the devil. James 4:7

- All mankind is to be submitted to those in authority over them. I Peter 2:13

- Angels and authorities are to be submitted to Christ. I Peter 3:22

- The younger are to be submitted to the older. I Peter 5:5

- Believers are to submit to their spiritual authorities. Hebrews 13:17

As you can see, submission is God's way of liberating leaders into a proper, healthy release of authority. More importantly, it is the method that God has chosen to align the entire universe under the headship and authority of his Son, Jesus Christ.

If submission is a God-idea, then it is also a Great Idea. We must embrace it with joy. Submission is not God's way of making us all miserable, but of releasing his full authority in us. Submission is God's way of setting us up for success in our position of authority.

That leads me to a probing question; Husband, father, employer, pastor, leader, are you personally submitted to authority? If not, you're leaving yourself vulnerable, unprotected and ineffective. Your effectiveness only comes when you're under authority. You have no right to expect submission from those you lead, if you are not under authority. Too often husbands demand submission from their wives, yet have never practiced it themselves.

Fortunately during the formative years of our marriage, God and my wife gave me enough grace until I learned how to exercise authority correctly. It has taken time, though, and I shed a lot of blood during the process, injuring my wife, family and congregation at times. I was sincerely trying to lead, but I was functioning without being under headship. I was exercising authority without being submitted to authority.

Biblical authority never demands, cajoles, suppresses or manipulates people. God-given authority is for the purpose of building people up, not tearing them down. II Corinthians 10:8 and 13:10.

My own submission to authority was tested in my younger years.

I was 12 or so when I learned a valuable lesson on submission. My dad, who had spent nearly all of his adult life working as a foreman for several California vineyards, was planting some grapevines in our backyard. As usual, he had me helping him. After digging a hole for the grapevine he asked me to hand him the grape stake. I had no idea that my reply would have such serious repercussions. "Get it yourself"? I said. Without saying a word, Dad laid the grapevine down, walked over to the grape stake and got it himself. Shortly thereafter I got it. Without warning, my dad lowered the board of education to the seat of understanding and I went flying across the yard. I want you to know that I got it! In more ways than one, I got it. I really understand the meaning of submission. I understand it first hand.

Would you believe that to this day I've never told anyone to, "get it yourself?" With one solid whack of a grape stake, I learned that submission is a valuable principle to remember. It has blessings if you do it and penalties if you don't.

Prior to the oft-quoted scripture from Ephesians 5:22 that says women should submit to their husbands, is the verse that provides the context for all the marriage scriptures that follow. Paul says in verse 21 that we are to submit to one another, out of reverence to Christ. Did you get that? Before demanding submission from your wife, men, you are to submit to one another.

Devi and I both believe strongly in the principle of submission.

She submits to me and I submit to her. And what determines our submission is not always an issue of who's right. In fact it rarely is. Neither of us portrays a melancholy hands-on-hip attitude of "okay, you're right, I'll submit to you." More often than not we want to honor the other by foregoing our own desire and pursuing theirs. Submission is not a forced give-in so peace can be maintained, but a decision to yield to the wisdom of the other.

Couples, especially when you both are leaders, need to understand that your authority is never weakened by submitting to your spouse. It is in fact strengthened.

Without doubt, one of the most poignant stories of submission comes from Jesus' encounter with the Roman centurion in Matthew 8. Jesus made it very clear to the centurion that because he, as a man of authority over 100 soldiers, was willing to submit himself to the authority of Jesus, his servant would be healed, his faith would be noted in Israel, and he would be included as a Gentile in the Kingdom of God.

That's not a bad reward for doing only one thing, being submitted to authority. The reward for you will be equally as great. Trust me. No, better yet, trust the Word of God. Your submission releases God to bless you.

CHAPTER FOUR

She says
we do it because we love him

SUBMITTED AND SATISFIED

DEVI It seems odd to me that submission is such a difficult concept for people to embrace, so difficult that this topic is rarely addressed in a direct way. Maybe it's because I grew up in a household where my mother respected my father. Now do not misunderstand and think that my spunky mother was a passive, permissive, and needy woman who never asserted herself. That was not the case.

Mother worked outside the home, paid the bills, and managed the household budget. Clearly, she was in love with my Dad, honored him, and submitted to him. We all knew who was boss.

Dad was boss, not because he was bossy, but because he was "Dad." There was never a question, or an option, to submit or not submit. We honored Dad by doing what he said. Not only did we do what he said but we cooked his favorite meals, endured endless baseball games on radio, and later television, even when he did not make us.

We did it because we loved him.

When I fell in love with Larry, responding to him in the same submissive way that I had related to my Dad was no different for me. It was natural. Early on, because my parents instilled a respect for authority in me, it was also natural to do what my schoolteacher said or to do what my employer said.

Submission is not to be feared. Submission is not just an action. It is a heart attitude of love and respect, honoring them as more important than yourself. It is natural when you have been taught obedience. However, if you were allowed as a child to disobey, and get your own way, you will have to work at developing a submitted heart.

A submitted heart does not have to prove itself. Remember, you never have to prove what you are; you only have to prove what you are not. You will argue less. If you are right, you do not have to prove it. Right, always proves itself, eventually. If you are wrong, submitting protects you. Your wrong will not consume you. Submission evens allows others to be wrong, without shame or blame.

Authority is everywhere. This authority principle is in operation the moment we are born. The human spirit must be surrendered to authority or it cannot survive in peace. When we resist authority, we are dissatisfied and miserable. Submitting to authority brings security and contentment. Submission releases rather than restricts.

Resisting authority takes so much negative energy. Think of a child who chooses to disobey. It takes so much energy to resist their parents' plea to "come here." They run. When they are caught, they fight, resist, throw a fit, cry and eventually collapse in exhaustion. Submitting would have been easier and more rewarding.

Since authority is a universal law, who am I to think that I can defy that law, and live in peace? Why would I even want to try to prove a universal principle wrong? I don't want to.

I choose to live in submission and be satisfied. What do you choose?

CHAPTER FIVE

He says criticism is always destructive.

THE CURSE OF CRITICISM

LARRY Though Paul failed to mention it in I Corinthians 12, I'm positive that many husbands and wives believe that one more gift should be added to the list of spiritual gifts, the gift of criticism. This is a gift that many couples begin manifesting shortly after they say, "I do." It consists of regular jabs, put-downs, belittling remarks, exposing faults, harping on weaknesses, constant condemnation, and miscellaneous nit-picking, until the silver-tongued condemner stands victor and the vanquished becomes a cowering failure, lacking any sense of value or self-confidence.

The gift of criticism is quite often exercised by just one of the marriage partners, who in the early stages of the marriage feels their calling in life is to change their mate. In order to make the necessary changes to see them transformed into their own image, it requires that the gifted spouse reveal, expose and magnify every perceived fault in the seemingly less-gifted partner. Unless other faults are exposed during the process, the ultimate result will be the perfect mate. Hallelujah!

Another valuable addition to the single use of the gift of criticism is when both partners are gifted at it. This double blessing is generally arrived at when both partners are adept at verbal boxing matches. In this scenario they try to out-do each other with snippets of sarcasm and tit-for-tat vocal jabs. Because neither one will back down when attacked, their goal is to verbally out spar the other with hurtful words until a knock out punch is achieved. Sometimes the boxing match can go on for months and even years. Unfortunately, the competition never really ends and the scars can last a lifetime.

Whether criticism comes mostly from one partner or both, the end result is the same—devastation. Neither spouse can rise to their full potential while being attacked by the other.

The gift of criticism is obviously the fruit of the human, carnal spirit, not the fruit of the Holy Spirit. What is it in human nature that is more prone to see and point out their partner's weaknesses rather than their strengths? Why would a husband destroy the self-worth in his wife, or a wife discredit her husband's sense of value? Why is it easier to defame a person than to encourage them? They both require the same amount of words.

THE CURSE OF CRITICISM

There is nothing more devastating than the unleashed, uncontrolled tongue. It can make failures out of even the most potential-filled partners. Do we really know how devastating continual criticism can be? No one can survive it. James, a writer in the New Testament, was right when he wrote in the third chapter of his letter that the tongue is set on fire in hell, and carries within its sting a world of iniquity.

I'm convinced that one of the reasons why we criticize our partners is that we're unhappy with ourselves. We don't like who we are, and our low self-esteem reveals itself in the way we treat our spouse. Any person who tears down another is insecure—bottom line.

When counseling young men who are considering making a marriage commitment to a young lady, I always ask one question. It may surprise you that my first question is never, "Is she born-again?" That's my second question. The first question always is, "When you're with her does she build you up or tear you down?" If she tears you down, run for your life. It's unlikely you will ever succeed in life or ministry with a spouse who berates you.

The same question is valid for a young lady. When you're in the presence of the man of your dreams, do you feel edified or beat down? The answer will tell you whether to proceed or flee. It doesn't matter if he acts like the world's most spiritual man, drop everything and run for your life. I've seen too many women destroyed by men who claimed to be a man of God, but as soon as they were married he turned into Attila the Hun and she became his emotional slave.

Self-righteousness can be another reason for criticizing our mates. A self-righteous spouse can berate their partner for not being spiritual enough. Regardless of how hard they try, the poor victim of spiritual harassment will never fully make the grade.

Self-righteous women will try to dominate a marriage through a variety of methods from manipulation to condemnation. Through subtle pressure to conform to her set of religious rules the wife continually prods the husband to read the Bible more, pray more, attend church more often and act more spiritual. All the time she is pressuring him to be the spiritual head of the house, she is in fact driving him further away. I'm sure these women believe that it's easier for them to make their husbands spiritual, than it is to trust the Holy Spirit. Or at least they feel the Holy Spirit could sure use their help.

In my experience, self-righteous men, unlike women, tend to use legalism, rather than manipulation or condemnation, to enforce their convictions. It's the letter of the law that counts. Grace is out of the question. I said it and that settles it. God and I are synonymous. You will be spiritual because "I said so!" The more self-righteous he becomes the more criticism is leveled at the wife and family members.

No one is exempt from this highly critical spirit.

Legalism is always heavy-handed. God is served not out of joy or love but out of obligation. All criticism comes in the form of condemnation. And pity the wife or children who love to have fun. Legalism considers fun to be a form of carnality and sin. I feel sorry for the wife and children who grow up under this self-righteous spiritual domination.

A third source of criticism comes in the form of perfectionism. The fastidious husband or wife can take their punctilious, flawless, meticulous demands into whole new realms of pain. They are masters of misery. They know how to make everyone miserable, including themselves. Their purist lifestyle always bleeds onto everyone and everything they come into contact with.

Praise God, I'm not a perfectionist, but I was at one time. I could pick out the speck in your eye a mile away. Through the telescopic lens of my judgmental attitude I could point out your faults without ever knowing you. I could criticize things that didn't even merit criticizing. I could find fault with your house, your kids, your hair, your lack of hair, your clothes, your dirty carpet, your mean, ugly dog, your dandruff and your lack of deodorant. I could criticize the way you walked, talked and flossed. I could criticize your theology. I could criticize your methodology. I could criticize your cosmology.

I could criticize your etymology. I could criticize your musicology. I could criticize your eschatology. And woe to the person who didn't have an "ology."

Then I got married. Oh, God help me! That was when I began to discover that perfectionism is a "sin." No, it's a SIN. The perfectionist is the ultimate of nit-pickers. They can find fault in everyone and everything.

For starters, my wife didn't put the lid on the toothpaste. In fact, she squeezed it from the middle. It was obvious she had never read the directions on the side of the box, a must for a perfectionist. And what was most egregious was the night I noticed my toothbrush was wet, before I used it. I was nearly ruptured before the rapture. "What? Just because you forgot your toothbrush at home doesn't mean you can use mine!"

Then came the day when I discovered she put the roll of toilet paper on the spool upside down. It was a dark day indeed. Can you imagine? I ask you, CAN YOU IMAGINE? Do you realize how traumatic that can be for a perfectionist? For men that are on the go, how can you go fast when the toilet paper is upside down?

Aren't you glad the day arrived when God showed me that he desires excellence, but not perfection? Yes, and so is everyone else. I've been born again, again.

THE CURSE OF CRITICISM

I was sitting in a restaurant, with my hand on the top of the booth cushion, when a man sitting at the booth behind me got up from his seat at the far side of the table and came over and tapped me on the shoulder. "You're about to touch my Mom." "Oh, I'm sorry," I responded, noticing for the first time his aged mom sitting behind me. "Did I touch your Mom?" "No," he replied, "but you're about to."

I had just come in contact with that lovely race of people who cannot tolerate imperfection in imperfect people. Human foibles, weaknesses, mistakes, sin and failure are inexcusable. Their standard is high. No, their standard isn't Jesus or the Bible, but themselves. If you don't measure up to their perfectionist requirements you are slated for their critical list. And once you get on their "list," it's hard to get off. The reason being, you'll probably keep committing the same unpardonable mistakes that put you there in the first place. Hell, for the perfectionist, is to discover that he's not perfect.

The bottom line, short and simple, is that perfectionism is a sin and needs to be repented of. No one is perfect, including the perfectionist. If your ultimate goal in life is to be a spiritual surgeon so you can remove the speck out of everyone else's eyes, especially your spouses, first take the log out of your own eye. Otherwise you lack the qualifications to perform the surgery.

Then there's the self-promotional spouse. In my opinion men, out of insecurity, are more culpable in this area. This is the man who deludes himself into thinking that the only way he can build himself up is to belittle his wife. And most of the time he does it on a subconscious level, not even knowing his motivation. But the results are public. The poor wife has to endure repeated humiliation and put-down in front of others so that his macho image can be publicly stroked.

What men must realize is that when they publicly degrade and humiliate their wives, they are destroying themselves as well. You cannot simultaneously build yourself up, while tearing your wife down. In Ephesians 5:28 Paul considers wife-hatred as self-hatred because you're one. What you do to her, you do to yourself. If you degrade her, you ultimately destroy yourself. It's that simple.

Now let's consider the controlling spouse. This issue is so important, however, other than including it now in the list of the common causes of criticism, I'll devote an entire chapter to it later. For now just understand that you cannot be a controlling spouse without frequently criticizing your mate.

For whatever reasons a spouse would belittle the other, it always boils down to one word, "self." Selfishness is the ultimate destroyer of marriage and leadership. Criticism in a marriage would quickly die out for lack of use if it weren't for selfishness raising its ugly head in the relationship.

There are two words that need to be banned from the English language because of their total inaccuracy. The words are "constructive criticism." In my opinion it's an oxymoron. It doesn't exist. Criticism is barbed, hurtful, insensitive, selfishly motivated and destructive. As soon as it is criticism it is no longer constructive. Criticism is always destructive. It is not motivated by love, but by a judgmental attitude on the part of the offender.

We all want to be corrected when we're wrong, even if we're as defensive as I am. But no one can continually endure criticism without it destroying their sense of value and self-worth.

So how do we exchange criticism for edification and encouragement? How can a person who is critical by nature change their personality to that of an encourager? God, after all, is a lifter of my head. There are plenty of ways to help a partner to grow into their full potential. Who better to help us be delivered from destructive habit patterns than a loving, sensitive spouse?

How can a destructive pattern of verbal abuse be broken? What is the antidote?

Remove the self-righteous log from your own eye. Jesus made it clear in Matthew 7:3-5 that if we wish to remove a speck from another's eye, we must first remove the log in our own eye. And it really works. When I find myself getting critical about something my wife is doing I stop and say to myself, "Larry, you're being critical about something that Devi is doing and totally oblivious to your own negative habits. If you'll change your negative habits first, then you can address her issues." The funny thing is that as soon as I start removing the log in my own eye I soon forget what was irritating me about her.

Turn the negative irritation into a positive attribute. You can always find positive in what was previously considered negative; look for it, it's there. Remember that God has not called you to change the other person. That's the job of the Holy Spirit. He has only called you to change yourself. That is recorded in Titus 1:1; Larry Titus 1:1, that is.

Choose to love. Love is a decision, not an emotion. Paul reminds us in I Corinthians: 13, that love remembers no wrongs, does not keep record of past hurts, is not envious of other's successes, and chooses to believe the best in a person. Peter also reminds us that love covers a multitude of sins.

Be patient with your spouse. God was patient with you. Extend to your partner the same grace that God has given you.

Speak only those words that build up the other person. In Ephesians 4:29 Paul reminds us to not allow any unwholesome, cancerous words to come out of our mouths, but only those words that are edifying and encouraging. Remember, we are not part of the destruction crew, but the construction crew. If our words do not build up our spouse, they are not to be used. Sometimes the most hateful words spoken by us are spoken to those we love the most. God help us!

Don't speak immediately when something has bothered you, or an issue has to be addressed. Let your emotions die down until you can see the other person's perspective. Don't give your spouse a piece of your mind if your opinion denigrates the other person. And remember, anytime you give a person a piece of your mind, it always leaves less for you.

I love to use my wife as an example of one who knows how to effectively use diplomacy and sensitivity in bringing things to my attention that need to be addressed and changed. I never feel that she is on the attack mode, but is genuinely interested in my welfare. And of course I, like many men, am defensive by nature, so it's important that we have spouses who know when and how to bring to our attention areas of concern.

I do not know of many successful leaders who have had spouses who were continually tearing them down. In fact I can't think of any. On the other hand, I can name hundreds of leaders whose wives or husbands were supportive and encouraging. If the spouse does not publicly and privately build up their mate, it matters little who else does. To have your wife or husband as the President of your Fan Club is the ultimate of blessings.

Sammy Jo Barbour, an inmate at the Iowa State Penitentiary, mailed me a parable that he had written after seeing Devi and me on Celebration, a television program hosted by Marcus and Joni Lamb from the Daystar Network, Dallas, TX:

PARABLE OF A ROSE

A certain man planted a rose and watered it faithfully. Before it blossomed, he examined it and saw the bud that would soon blossom, but noticed thorns upon the stem and thought, "How can any beautiful flower come from a plant burdened with so many sharp thorns?"

Saddened by his thought, he neglected to water the rose and before it was ready to bloom, it died.

So it is with many people. Within every soul there is a rose. The God-like qualities planted in us at birth growing amid the thorns of our faults. Many of us look at ourselves and see only the thorns, the defects. We despise ourselves, thinking that nothing good can possibly come from us. We neglect to water the good within us and eventually it dies. We never realize our potential.

Some people do not see the rose within themselves. Someone else might show it to them. One of the greatest gifts a person can possess is to be able to reach past the thorns and find the rose within others. This is the characteristic of love—to look at a person and know their true faults, accepting that person into your life, while recognizing the nobility in their soul. Help them to realize that they can overcome their faults. If we show them the rose, they will conquer their thorns. Only then will they blossom many times over. Within every soul there is a rose.

Praise God for my leader/wife who has spent her life choosing to ignore my thorns and cultivate my roses.

CHAPTER FIVE

THE CURSE OF CRITICISM

DEVI Larry amazes me. Obviously he has used an oxymoron to captivate your attention. Using sarcasm, for the sake of emphasis, is one way of communicating a poignant truth. A truth that is essential for you to embrace, especially when leaders live together. The truth is criticism in all forms is a curse, not a gift! It is impossible for anyone to reach their goals in life and live under the dark cloud of criticism. Criticism creates self-doubt. No one continues to achieve when self-doubt prevails.

I wanted my husband to succeed. He was in full time ministry when we married and I felt honored to be a minister's wife. I must admit that I had a bit of fantasy about the life of a minister's family. I saw his profession up there along with the mayor of the city, the doctors and the lawyers. It was not long after we accepted our first pastorate, however, that I learned differently. Somehow, the important person that I thought I was married to was a target for criticism. Not only was he criticized, but so was I and so were our children.

I soon learned that my defense to the attempts of others to destroy my husband's success was to build him up when others were tearing him down. It's not that I did not see his faults; it's just that his virtues were so much greater. I was the one who had power in his life to drive out self-doubt.

If he succeeds, I am blessed. If he fails, I suffer. Why then would I choose to create or enforce self-doubt by pointing out his faults?

Words have power! My favorite scripture—a guide for my life—is in Ephesians: *Let no unwholesome word proceed from your mouth, but only such a word as is good for edification according to the need of the moment, that it may give grace to those who hear.* Ephesians 4:29. I believe it is in everyone's carnal nature to find fault in others. This is a low level of living. However, when we truly walk in the Spirit, we will choose to overcome carnal ways and apply the truth to our lives. The more secure you become in Christ, the easier it is to build others up.

Unwholesome words are words that keep others from being whole. The destructive wife is a wife who constantly tears down her husband. She nags, she belittles, and berates.

It is so embarrassing and uncomfortable to be in a social situation with other couples that punch and jab one another with words. The atmosphere becomes stifling as if you can't breathe. Certainly you know not to laugh, you really want to cry. How sad it is for love to be punctured with such cruel and unkind words.

The initial consequences of criticizing your husband in front of your children will cause them to disrespect their father. However, as they get older, they will disrespect you.

A young woman who was raised by her mother, because of divorce, told this story to me. She explained that her mother reported her father as being an awful, demonic-like man. Because of bitterness between her parents, she was deprived from having a relationship with her father. Only later, as she became an adult, did she reunite with her Dad. She found him to be a practical, hard working and care-giving person. Initially, she saw her mother as a victim. Now, she questions her truthfulness. She understands that her mother is critical, self-righteous, and manipulative. She lovingly maintains a relationship with both parents but clearly sees the devastating results of criticism.

Criticism never reaps good consequences. What you hoped to achieve will always turn on you. Everyone loses.

CHAPTER 6

ME MACHO

LARRY You can nearly hear the grunts of Tarzan as he swings from tree limb to tree limb. Finally he hits the ground with a thud and bellows out his famous yell. "Ah-ee-ah-ee-ah-ee." Then he turns to Jane, pounding his chest, yelling, "Me macho, me the leader." Then of course, Jane, having read Ephesians 5:21 willingly submits to her spiritual stud with a dismissive, "Of course you are honey. And I humbly submit to your spiritual authority."

As the pendulum of leadership swings back and forth between the husband and wife, most of the time it maintains a healthy balance by both of the spouses. Each knows their respective areas of ability and expertise, and yields to the other when it is theirs. However, on occasion Tarzan shows up. You can tell him by his dented chest, having been made concave by his macho ravings and chest beatings.

This kind of man knows strong, unilateral leadership, but doesn't know the give and take of normal leadership. He only knows the take side. He maintains authority by fear tactics, fits of anger, financial control, intimidation, secrecy, moodiness, selfishness, and suppression of his wife and children. He has absolute dominance over the home environment. He is free to extend emotional and/or physical abuse, and an occasional great decision that makes him look better than he really is.

Unfortunately, domineering male leadership keeps their followers anemic and weak. It is critical for all strong male leaders to share leadership with the rest of the family members, and in particular, their spouse. It is not only necessary for a healthy balance in the home, which produces healthy family members, but it is necessary for the man himself so he can become all that God intends for him.

The opposite of the dominant male leader is the sheepish, wimpish, nondescript, milque-toast, abdicating, cringing, effete, weak, indecisive man. His most quoted response is, "Yes, dear." This man doesn't swing from trees or bushes. Swinging from trees is too dangerous, and romping through bushes can create a rash. He might consent to pruning them, if he has gloves to wear, so the pruning shears don't chaff his hands. You know how much lotions cost these days.

Virtually, all of these good, but timid men, have a tremendous fear of their wives. This immobilizes them from making any effective decisions, and in turn win the respect of their wives, which both of them desire. In fact, because he fears making the wrong decision, he will most likely not make any.

I heard an example of this type of man several years ago, told in typical apocryphal form by a preacher wanting to exaggerate a point. It was said that St. Peter, in an attempt to screen the newly arrived candidates into heaven, instructed all the men who had not been hen-pecked by their wives to stand in one particular reserved section in the celestial city. From that area they would be assigned their mansion. All obediently complied by moving into their holding room, with the exception of one little timid man who was cowering in the corner. "Why aren't you standing with the rest of the men?" the revered Apostle demanded. "Because my wife told me to stand over here."

It's cute, if you haven't heard it before, but it speaks a truth that appears to fit this generation of men. Most were raised by mothers, grandmothers, or aunts, and grew up without having a strong pant leg to hold on to, and a male role model to be mentored by.

I find the head-drooped, defeated men that fit this description more sad than pathetic. We are rearing a generation of passive men that desperately need role models. We need strong, spiritual, balanced, sensitive male leaders, who will take these men under their coat tails and help them escape the paralysis and pain of this life-style.

While there are several examples of week, timid, and diffident leaders in the Bible, it doesn't seem to be the type of man that God is drawn to. The reason is because a man who is retiring and shy rarely demonstrates the authority that is needed to represent God. In the same way, however, the Lord rarely calls upon the Tarzan types either. One refuses to use authority, while the other only knows how to abuse it. Either extreme is reason for disqualification.

Elijah, the man who became John the Baptist's model and the one in Malachi 4:5 that the prophet commands us to emulate, was another "Man's Man!" He came onto the scene with a zeal for the Lord that both decimated Jezebel's prophets, and defied Ahab's blasphemies. His word had enough power to stop the heavens from raining for three and a half years, and enough compassion to feed a widow and her son, so they could live through the famine.

Resident in Elijah was a personality that could be as tough as nails when dealing with a tyrant and as soft as velvet when caring for a despairing mother. Don't feel that you have to make a choice between being all bluster and bravado, or soft, retiring and aloof. God wants you balanced. He's looking for leaders who are both authoritative and gentle, commanding and compassionate. Your sword needs to be sharp on one side and gentle on the other.

When John the Baptist arrived on the scene hundreds of years later, Jesus said that he had come in the spirit of Elijah. To prove his point, Jesus asked the crowd a very probing question: *What did you go out into the desert to see? A reed swayed by the wind? If not, what did you go out to see? A man dressed in fine clothes? No, those who wear expensive clothes and indulge in luxury are in palaces. But what did you go out to see?"* Luke 7:24-26.

Jesus is actually asking the populace if they came out of their towns and villages to witness an effeminate preacher. It is obvious by His rhetorical question that He was not looking for a reply. When God asks a question, He is never looking for a reply, only a response. He wanted the crowds to take notice that John the Baptist was not effeminate or soft. So what was His point? Simple! God is not going to send out a messenger to introduce Him who doesn't properly represent Him. Men are not attracted to timid, pathetic, mealy-mouthed men. Neither is God and neither are women.

A woman may be initially attracted to the sensitivity of a timid man before they are married, but if after marriage she discovers that his sensitivity is a cover-up for an indecisive, sheepish nature, she will immediately lose respect for him. So will everyone else.

Who would you go out into the wilderness to see? Not much

draws me to the wilderness to see anyone. I might go to a national forest, to the Pacific Ocean, or to a Caribbean Island to see someone. If I go to the wilderness to hear, or see someone, it will be to have an encounter with John the Baptist, Jesus, Elijah, or someone else that exudes authority. They will also command respect, demand repentance, and know when it's the right time to back off and yield authority to one who has authority over them. Otherwise I'm not available.

I also believe that when Jesus comes again, His selection process will probably be the same as it was when He came the first time. He will choose men who will properly reflect who He is. These men will carry the spirit of Elijah and they are not afraid to forcefully advance the Kingdom of God.

When Jesus came onto the scene, His natural authority distinguished Him from the teachers of the law and endeared Him to the crowds. After all, when as a people you've endured centuries of tyrannical rule, a man who leads by example, rather than force, is immediately recognized.

Yet the Leader of all leaders knew how to be humble, quiet, sensitive, compassionate, and non-argumentative. Only once did his zeal become overtly intense and that was for the purpose of cleansing his father's house. What a man. What a man's man. What a perfect role model for the rest of us.

I resent the pictures from the middle ages that have made Jesus look effeminate and beautiful. The paintings were created by artists using hired models posing as the man Jesus. Of course, since none of these artists had actually seen Jesus, they had to hire stand-ins that fit their imagination of what Jesus looked like. Obviously they had never read Isaiah's description of Christ in Isaiah 53, as indescribably homely, or that of John the Beloved in Revelation 1, with his flaming eyes and voice that sounded like rushing waters. No effeminacy here. Their caricatures stuck and for hundreds of years we have had images of Jesus in every home and bookstore that make him look more like a salesman in a department store cosmetic counter, than a carpenter with rough, splintered hands.

I just can't imagine Jesus offering me a limp-wristed handshake when He returns in glory, can you? Not from the one who will rule the nations of the world with an iron rod.

By the way, if someone suggests that you should get in touch with your feminine side, tell them that the only feminine side you have is your wife, and that you're in touch with her everyday. Literally.

It's hard for mild-mannered men who are gentle and laid-back by nature, to relate to Jesus' zeal in cleansing the temple. Or another example, John the Baptist ranting at the river with grasshoppers clogging his esophagus, or to Elijah calling down fire from heaven on the prophets of Baal, then sending them to an early grave. Now we do have a lot of men more than happy to engage in those exploits, with or without the Spirit leading them. But for the man with a meek disposition it is just not natural for him to be forceful. I relate. I'm such a man. I prefer staying distant, somewhat reclusive, uncomfortable with anything that demands confrontation, and nervous as all get out when it comes to assuming authority. How are we supposed to lead in this foreign and uncomfortable environment?

In the Introduction to this book, I described how I lead by conviction and obligation. Both of these motivations come from the Word of God. I have a deep conviction that God has called all men to be heads, and therefore I must lead. I also know, Biblically, that God has delegated me, and all men, to extend his authority; therefore, I am obligated to exercise authority, whenever it is needed. It is my job to do so. I can't say that I have ever enjoyed being authoritative, but it's a responsibility that I accept for the sake of maintaining unity, peace and harmony in the marriage and family.

How I exercise authority is another story. I've tried at times to use authority in a high-handed, rancorous way, but it isn't me. The approach that I feel most comfortable with, and that fits my personality best, is to deliver the mandate with little volume and emotions under control. I want as much as possible to understand the heart of the person or persons that are being affected.

Though he may have done it, I just can't imagine Joshua standing on a hill top in Ephraim, screaming at the top of his lungs with veins protruding from his neck, "Listen to me you bunch of rebellious, rapscallion, rogue Jews. I'm sick and tired of you vacillating between gods. I've decided what I'm going to do, and if you don't want to go to Sheol, you'd better do it too. As for me and my house, we're going to serve the Lord. Did you hear that kids? Well, if you'd shut up and stop playing around with your slingshots, you would have heard me. Now go back to the tent and eat your bagels."

I think Joshua's last words were uttered with pure conviction. They didn't require a lot of volume, because Joshua had already made up his mind that there was only one course of action for him and his family. He would make sure that they followed it. There were no options, and there was no way anyone could change his mind. Leading by pure conviction and demonstrated by example is a great way to inspire others to follow you.

My favorite way to dispense authority is by example. I must be willing to submit to those whom God has placed in authority over me, if I am to expect others to obey my authority. However, when I demand things from my wife and children that I do not abide by, it results in hypocrisy in me and rebellion in them.

There are times when the temple of men's homes must be put back in order by the cleansing action of discipline and authority. At those times Jesus won't come down in the flesh to do it for them. They must put things in order themselves. They must take upon themselves that part of Jesus' nature that is both compassionate and confrontational. The steel-willed conviction inside them must be as strong and determined as that of Joshua: *As for me and my house, we will serve the Lord.* No ifs, ands or buts about it; abdication to the wife's leadership at times like this are out of the question.

God hasn't called men to be demanding, dictatorial, chest-thumping Jane suppressors. He has called them to be men of action, decisiveness, conviction, and character-charged Kingdom-chasers. Jesus' glowing compliment of John the Baptist, the one whom He called the *greatest born of women*, was that he *took the Kingdom by force.* In the same verses in Matthew 11:11-15 He then identified him with the spirit of Elijah. You don't need to wear garments of scratchy camel hair, eat grasshoppers, and live in the desert to fulfill God's purpose as an Elijah man. But you do have to be a man of conviction. A man who refuses to bow to this generation's view of a man that ranges all the way from hairy-chested machismo types on steroids, to androgynous women wannabees seeking breast implants. This generation has been so emasculated, there needs to be a new definition of manhood, and it must come from the Bible and men who model the Biblical example.

We who live in the final days of Gentile occupation, before Christ's return, must learn to move in that same spirit of Elijah. We have a Biblical mandate in Malachi 4:5, to come in the spirit of Elijah to restore Godly leadership in homes. We have a mandate by the King of Kings in Matthew 11 to forcefully advance the Kingdom of God in the spirit of Elijah. We must make up a new generation of Elijah men. Men committed to putting their families before both job and church; men faithful to their wives, examples to their children, role models for godliness to the young men of the world, and most of all men of courage, who are not afraid to stand against the kingdom of darkness. It cannot be accomplished through bombastic dictatorial dictums, but with a spirit of humility and brokenness.

It was said of Jesus that He was not argumentative, never raised the volume of His voice in the streets, and yet was so gentle that a smoking wick He would not extinguish, nor break a bent reed. Matthew 12:18-21. This is what I call a "man's Man." This is the kind of leader that others will automatically follow, and the nations will put their trust in. Jesus was obviously not driven by insecurity or a need to prove Himself, but was confident in whom the Father had called Him to be.

Men, regardless of your leadership style, or the bend of your personality, it is still imperative that you lead. Don't abdicate your leadership responsibilities. This is what it means to forcefully advance the Kingdom of God. After all, when Christ returns to establish his Kingdom on this earth, we want to be part of His leadership team. So it's time to start practicing for prime-time.

CHAPTER SIX

She says me macho tee...not really

ME MACHOETTE

DEVI Unfortunately, the attitude of many women in leadership today is one of competition with men. In order to finally seize a fair share of power in the male-dominated business world, or church world, and gain personal notoriety and respect, many women have felt it necessary to speak in borrowed voices—voices of men. They have convinced themselves, that they should dress in business suits, sacrifice nurture and sensitivity, be assertive, and speak tough in order to be heard.

In truth, this kind of action dilutes the impact of female leadership rather than strengthening it. The lie of early feminism is that there is one way, a guys way, and for women to lead they must lead with the male macho style. By now, generations have passed since the push for equal rights. Now, having lived decades, sacrificing our femininity, it is time to reemphasize our human birthright to cooperation, sensitivity, and empowering of others. This is what we are really good at.

Both women and men stand to gain if business people, businesses, churches and families adopt a *tender* strategy. A book written on this subject, Tender Power by Sherry Suib Cohen, clearly demonstrates, through personal stories and research, the impact that tender leadership can have in your professional and private world.

The true female influence has changed domineering masculine management styles to a more family environment of co-operation or team building. This is called the new model of leadership. Books are written on it and corporations are benefiting from it. But is it really new? Not for women. We have just moved away from what is really natural and comfortable.

Leadership is about empowering others: your husband, your children, your friends, your colleagues, and your associates. When the people around you are empowered, so are you. Women have been empowering others since the time of Eve. It is an ancient female trait.

Trying to do, and to be everything, building yourself up, becomes a heavy load. In the scriptures, Jesus said it this way, *"Come to me all of you who are heavy laden and I will give you rest. Take my yoke upon you and learn from me for I am TENDER and humble."* Matthew 11:28,29

Returning to TENDER will lift the load that you often carry. There is power in just being nice! So what is POWER and what is TENDER?

Plain old power, the kind that is usually practiced in a competitive environment, often a male dominated environment, has some of these characteristics: It is directive. It's self-protective. It's not connecting. It values the outcome over caring. It is about facts not feelings. It is competitive. Some descriptive words for power are: vigor, potency, pressure, energy, strength, and ability to influence.

Tender power, on the other hand, can be revolutionary and equally valuable to men and women, and can be adopted by both if you do not fear trying something new. Some descriptive words for tender are: vulnerable, soft, empathic, sensitive, loving, gentle, considerate, merciful, passionate, generous, and kind.

Although the descriptive words for power, and for tender, are absolute opposites look how empowering they become when they are yoked together.

Sensitive strength

Empathic leadership

Loving force

Considerate ability to influence

Gentle pressure

Tarzan and Jane need each other. Tender power swinging together in unity puts *heart* in what you do—heart in your business, in your ministry, in your family, in your marriage.

Tender power is about partnerships. The war on sexes, viciously or subtly competing with one another, is not ordained. Instead of the "Me Tarzan, you Jane" model, husbands and wives in leadership can hold the rope together. Sometimes that means cook together, clean together, stuff envelopes together, and share courteously, supporting one another in whatever they need to succeed.

Tender power is about empowering others—a generosity of spirit that passes knowledge on to those on the lower rungs of your ladder.

Tender power is about empathy, the human ability to put one's self in another's shoes.

Larry is such an example of tender power in my life. He has encouraged me and corrected me; both are aspects of leadership. When he corrects me, it is with sensitivity and empathy. If I feel embarrassed, he loves me and nurtures me, until I have regained my courage.

When I approach him with a "righteous appeal," pleading for him to change his mind, I enter his male ego with generous amounts of praise. Knowing that defensiveness is a vulnerability for him, I state my concern, correction, or conviction and do not demand a decision.

I then submit my appeal and surrender the outcome. I give him time to respond.

When we empower one another with tenderness, we grow in personal esteem and security. It feels good to be kind. I feel better about myself. When coercion comes by aggression everyone looses. I feel unfulfilled and guilty and he feels insecure and angry.

Men and women, husbands and wives, do not be afraid to be gentle. Power combined with tenderness accentuates your power. It doesn't diminish it.

CHAPTER SEVEN

They say beware of leadership...

CAUTION ZONE~WATCH FOR RED FLAGS

LARRY and DEVI   There are a lot of hazards along the leadership highway, so it's time to post some caution markers and red flag zones. Be advised, your effectiveness as a leader depends on how you steer your life and marriage through this rough terrain. These areas of concern can derail the loftiest vision. And no one is immune from the deadly potential.

Solomon warned us in his Song of Songs that we were to watch out for the little foxes that ruin the vines. But these cautions are more than cute little foxes nibbling at young vines. They are roaring lions of destruction, capable of destroying the greatest of leaders and toppling the tallest leadership towers.

RED FLAGS

The Trauma of Transitions

Benjamin Franklin said that two things in life are inevitable: death and taxes. He's right. And I've got another inevitability that I could add to his list—transition. Changes are inevitable and they always carry the potential for rocking the boat at best or capsizing it at worst. When one of the leadership partners goes through a transition, it will always affect the other. And quite often, if you think about it, the one that is most deeply affected by the change is not the one who has made the decision but the one who has to conform to the decision that was not theirs.

It is impossible to experience changes in plans, vision, goals, locations, positions, occupations or staff without an attending emotional trauma. Even when you know it is God's will for the change, it is still traumatic. It will take time to adjust. It will take time to sort out the various emotions involved. It can be painful. You need to understand that life can be very unsettling at those times.

Changes will quite often include separation from friends and family. Sometimes you will be thrust into a totally new and unfamiliar environment.

Occasionally it will mean an income loss, and you know how

insecure that can make you feel.

Transition can result from a bad decision that brings negative consequences. At other times the change can initially look troublesome only to discover later that it was one of the best decisions that you've ever made. Retrospection can at times be very educational. "Time will tell," is more than a trite expression. It's a very accurate way of assessing your past to affect your future.

Can you imagine how the wives must have felt when the 12 disciples abruptly dropped the news that they were leaving their fishing boats to follow a total stranger named Jesus from Nazareth? "Oy veh, are you losing your mind?" In hindsight we can see how absolutely correct their decision was. I think we can correctly assume, however, that their wives didn't see it that way. All they knew was that they were losing their husbands, the father of their children, and their income.

Unilateral leadership decisions can be relationally dangerous. The non-deciding spouse can feel betrayed, not valued, abandoned and left out of the decision. Early in our marriage, I unilaterally made decisions, leaving my wife out of the loop. I thought I knew what "God" wanted and made a headship decision, forgetting that it should have been a "leaders"-ship decision. That left my wife emotionally drained with a need to deal with the trauma of transition without having been part of the process. I knew what I was doing and why

I was doing it, but I hadn't communicated with her. Though I didn't include her in the decision, I expected her to be part of the consequences. We both suffered because of my inconsideration.

Communication is absolutely essential during transition times. Talk, talk, talk, talk, and more talk.

Time must pass for perspective to be gained. Even if your decisions are dead right on, there still must be a time lapse built into the transition so you can see the whole picture and gain a clear understanding of the outcome. Both of you will need time to sort out the details. Transitions should not be rushed, and you need to understand that from the get-go.

The same thing is true when transitions are caused by a crisis such as the death of a spouse, business partner, or family member. In these situations time is always your ally. Watch God use time to heal the wounds of unwanted transitions.

I've never yet experienced a change in jobs, homes, administrative adjustments, positions, or employees without some form of emotional trauma. Even when I knew it was God's will, it has still been traumatic. The nature of the beast is that change is unsettling, insecure, and at times painful. But it generally always produces good results if we just wait for it.

I've cried for weeks when leaving friends and family to follow God to a new location. I've gone through huge times of self-doubt every time I have resigned from a church to pursue another ministry. Changes in staff are inevitably disconcerting and unnerving as well. Our flesh loves the security of the familiar. Disturb the status quo and you set yourself up for pain. But change is not only inevitable, it is necessary, and so is the pain of change. God is the only one who does not change. The rest of us must.

When Business Overtakes Intimacy

Years ago I heard of a camel that sought refuge from the raging sand storm inside the tent of his Bedouin master. "Good master, may I just put my head into your tent so I can escape the fury of the storm." "Okay," replied the master, "but only your head." After a few hours the camel prodded his master again. "Good master, may I put just my front feet into the tent and escape the stinging sand that is so painful to my legs." "Okay," the gracious host responded. "But you can only put in your head and front legs."

You of course know the rest of the story. The camel was unwilling to protect just his front quarter so continued to nag his master until he eventually was entirely inside the tent. The story doesn't end there, however. The final camel communication wasn't a request for additional protection from the storm, but a demand that the master leave the tent so the camel could have all the space for himself. What started as a casual request from a polite dromedary eventually became a command from a usurping tyrant.

So it is with business or should I say busyness. It is never satisfied occupying a secondary place in your life. It wants everything, including quiet and intimate times with your spouse, all free time, your days off, your kid's ball games, your worship times, your prayer hour, and even your sleep at night. It knows no boundaries. Its relentless pursuit of every waking hour makes it one of the most ruthless enemies of your marriage and is the ultimate of thieves. Leaders are vulnerable.

Business can be a tyrant. Who was the wise man that said when you're lying on your death bed you won't be thinking of how you could have worked more, but you will question why you hadn't devoted more time to your wife and family.

Don't forfeit your intimate times with your husband or your wife for additional hours at work or the office. And above all, don't give the time that your spouse deserves to office workers, especially those of the opposite sex. The devil is working over time trying to get people who have contracted and covenanted themselves in marriage to begin looking to others for the intimacy that only their spouse can provide.

Go home to your spouse. Leave the office workers and business acquaintances. They need to be home with their families. Take time off to be with your spouse. Leave work early to attend your kids sporting events. Cultivate quiet times with your husband or wife. Provide for intimacy. If you don't, someone else will. And that "someone" has the potential to destroy your marriage, family and future. Intimacy is too precious to entrust with someone other than your spouse.

Women Or Men Who Intrude Into Intimacy

This point sounds exactly like the previous one. But it isn't. God is a jealous God. He is unwillingly to share you with any one or any thing other than him. He desires an intimate relationship with you. And so it is with marriage.

God wants you to have intimate times with your spouse that no one else has privy to. Don't share with others intimate details that only your spouse should know. Don't give away pieces of your heart that are pre-owned. They belong only to your mate. The office workers, no matter how sympathetic they might sound, have no right to hear or know the private details of your life.

And your business or professional acquaintances do not deserve, nor should they have, those special times when you need to be with your spouse without the company of others.

Men, don't be tempted to share marriage problems with an

understanding woman in the office. A daily, intimate discussion at the water cooler can quickly turn into a dalliance and then divorce. You not only risk your marriage and family, but also your heart. Adultery has deadly consequences. And remember, Jesus said that adultery starts in the heart, not the bed.

I don't believe it's wise to take women to lunch or meet them for counseling without your wife or others being present. I don't trust my flesh for one minute and I don't trust yours either. The flesh is the flesh, period!

Women, you have the same obligation to avoid any form of intimacy with a man who is not your spouse. Remember, the man who may be sensitive to your needs during your secret lunch-time or after-hours conversations is the same man that is insensitive to the needs of the woman that he is married to now.

When To Take Off The Business Hat

I know it's hard to do, but when you leave the office you need to "leave" the office. And I mean, leave your business at the office. Don't bring it home with you. Turn your cell phones off, talk about other things than business, put on your home hat and leave everything else at the office for tomorrow.

Your voice tone should change from demanding and challenging to understanding and inviting. Your spouse needs to be addressed as an equal and not a subordinate. Your staff are paid to honor you as their boss, but no such privilege exists at home, so don't be "bossy."

Enter your home with peace. Approach your mate and family members in sensitivity and considerateness. Your wife is your equal, so condescending words and actions are not acceptable. Wives, your husband is your head, not your son, so he needs to be treated with respect and honor. Titles, projects and professionalism can be picked up tomorrow morning when you arrive at work, but until then, your family would prefer the real you and all of you.

It's easy at times for a leader/partner to forget that their spouse is not their secretary, assistant, or domestic lackey. "Honey, just tell me what'd you like for me to do. I'd love to help you, but I would prefer you approach me with a question or request rather than a demand. I'm your other half, not your paid staff."

Don't Base Your Identity on the Success or Failure of Your Current Project or Job.

What if I fail? It's okay if you fail. Remember, the road to success is paved with stones of failure. Don't base your self-worth on whether or not you succeed.

God loves you for who you are, not what you do. If you have all the money, degrees, power, acclaim and wisdom in the world, God would still not be impressed. So the issue isn't whether or not God will approve of you, is it? The issue is whether you will approve of yourself if you fail to reach your goal.

Your self-worth must be based on what God thinks of you, not what you accomplish in life. Promise yourself that you will not require of yourself perfection, but only that you will try. Then be happy with the results.

Jesus never judged Peter for falling beneath the waves when he attempted to walk to Jesus on the water, but he did judge the others for not getting out of the boat. True failure is staying in the boat.

Watch Out For The Major Destroyer of Marriages

I know you're waiting for me to say the "A" word, but adultery is not my major concern at this point. Lest someone think that I'm minimizing the potential dangers of affairs, let me assure you the reason I mentioned it above was to emphasize how deadly it is. But there is something far more subtle and deadly, and that is selfishness. In my opinion selfishness is at the root of all marital difficulties.

After 44 years of ministry, with 34 of them while I was serving as Senior Pastor, I have never, let me repeat, never had any couple come into my office for counseling where selfishness was not the major issue. There are always surface issues such as money, infidelity, or lack of communication, but they inevitably boil down to selfishness.

Selfishness can be easily identified by one attitude and it's, "Me first." If you were to consider the other person as more important than yourself, as Philippians 2:3 says you must do, selfishness would then no longer be an issue. Change your, "me first" attitude to, "you first." Selfishness would diminish and die over night if you were to take such a stance.

Selfishness will destroy any marriage, relationship, family, church or nation. Nothing is more deadly. The crooner who sang, "I want it my way," didn't know how deadly his suggestion was. Getting things "my way," destroys any possibility of success in life. Plus, it denies the very essence of the Gospel that puts God first, others second and you last. I have a suggestion; let's write a new song entitled, *I'll Do It Your Way!*

CHAPTER EIGHT

He says — she is my better two-thirds

LIVING WITH A LEADER

LARRY In the Introduction of this book I described how my wife came out of the womb as a leader. It's as natural for her as breathing. She leads me, herself, her staff, the people on the plane, anyone standing in line at the grocery check-out, the traffic, the police, the yard men, the construction crew, and most of all, tens of thousands of women across the nation. And I'm proud as punch of her. The greater her release and exposure, the happier I am.

I believe that God has gifted and graced me with a few leadership skills, but nothing compared to those of my wife. I would be totally intimidated if it weren't for two facts: Devi never displays a one-upmanship or superior attitude toward me, and she is always supportive of my vision. I know that a secure leader would probably not need those qualities coming from his other half, but for me I need them.

There are two major things that factor into my response to her leadership and keep me from being negative or resentful:

Number one, I'm comfortable in who God made me to be, so I'm not intimated. I love what God has called me to do. I'm happy as a clam to preach, teach, disciple men, and invest in global ministries and leaders. I get tired even thinking of doing what she does. Devi moves at a killer pace and I move at a snail pace. She wants to have fun, fun, fun, while I can hardly wait to slip away and take a nap. She wants to sit on the front pew, even when visiting a strange church, and I want to sit under the pew. She loves the limelight and I prefer lime-lite. Most of the time she needs a tranquilizer and I need a shot of adrenaline.

Secondly, I'm blessed to see her excel. It doesn't make me envious or jealous when she is called on to speak at a larger conference than me. I'm proud to see her moving in her gifts.

Years go I had a pastor call me to see if Devi and I could come and speak at his church. When I responded that I was available, but Devi wasn't, he replied, "That's okay, she was the one I really wanted." Thanks a lot buddy. No Christmas card for you this year. Just kidding, sort of.

I'm blessed to see her blessed. I have a tremendous pride in her accomplishments. I'm as fascinated by her as others are. I don't mind seeing her get all the attention. In fact, I'd rather see her receive the accolades than me.

You've heard many men introduce their wives using the hackneyed phrase, "I'd like you to meet my better half." I introduce Devi by saying, "I'd like you to meet my better three-quarters." Isn't that cute? I thought of it all by myself. No, the reason I say that is because I really believe it. She really does pull three quarters of the leadership weight; and that's not being condescending, it's true. Devi can lead circles around me. And I enjoy the whirl of her activity. Like the tail of the comet, she pulls me into the gravitational force of her vision, so we can enjoy the ride together. Without her I'd be spinning off into space.

How many men live with a woman whose leadership skills out perform theirs, yet have never experienced the joy of seeing them blessed? I would suspect a lot. Probably a greater percentage than we could imagine.

I could never understand leaders who get jealous, envious and restricting, when their disciples became better than they. That should be the greatest of compliments, when the one you have invested in excels you. I love to see my wife and kids go further than I have ever gone. It brings honor to me when I can rejoice in their accomplishments.

The final prayer of Jesus in John 17 was that his disciples experience the glory that the Father had given Him. The glory that the Father had shared with the Son from eternity past was now being passed down to his disciples. A great leader gladly shares his victories with those coming behind him. An insecure leader fears his spotlight will have to include others and is unwillingly to do so.

I think my attitude toward my wife, in my lack of resentment for her leadership skills, and in my desire to promote her and see her blessed, came from two sources. My contentment with my own gifts, and the joy and satisfaction that I have in my calling definitely came from my mother, Rachel Titus. She was an incredibly gifted speaker and teacher and loved what she did. She kept her suitcase packed at all times and could hardly to wait to board the plane for her next appointment.

I love what I do. With the kids out of the house, and no longer carrying the pastoral responsibilities of a local congregation, my pace quickens and my spirit brightens at the thought of boarding another plane and preaching to a new congregation. Why would I begrudge my wife's success when I'm so happy with mine?

My ability to rejoice at Devi's achievements definitely comes from my dad's side of the family. I caught him in the Mall one day bragging on me to a total stranger. "You should hear my son. He's just as good as Billy Graham." While I enjoyed the compliment, I was under no illusion. To compare Billy Graham and me stretches the imagination to gargantuan proportions, but that didn't matter to Dad. In Dad's eyes I was right up there in the rarified air with the greatest evangelist on earth.

Dad was a promoter of people, and it started in his own home. To Dad, my Mom was the greatest preacher on earth, and I was right up there with Billy Graham. I never remember Dad even insinuating that he resented Mom or anyone else's success.

Dad treated my Mother with both deference and reverence. He knew how to decrease so she could increase, to step down so she could step up. In fact, he did this literally when he would introduce her to speak. Though my Dad couldn't preach a lick in the road, he would always introduce Mom before she spoke. You would think that one greater than Margaret Thatcher was about to take the podium. Mom would then walk regally to the pulpit, take the microphone and reciprocate by honoring dad in the same way in which she had been honored.

Dad was a firm believer in chivalry. He was honor-bound to open the door for Mom any time she approached. In fact she wrote a poem that was read at his funeral in 1972.

Wait For Me At the Door

Parting enriches the golden hours
Of memories I hold in store;
The many times you gently spoke,
"Wait, I'll open the door."

Chivalry was asserted in declining years,
As it was in days of yore;
"You be a lady and wait for me,
I'm your man and I'll get the door."

Hurriedly your hand was laid on the door
And swinging the portals wide,
You gently ushered me safely through,
Then fell in step by my side.

I'll miss your love and comfort
And your words of encouragement more;
But the thing that I'll miss the most,
You're not here to open the door.

I must learn to open my own doors
And walk on bravely through
To meet whatever lies beyond
Without the nearness of you.

For heavens realm has beckoned
And you have gone before,
But when I arrive, you'll surely say,
"Wait, I'll open the door."

Don't send Saint Peter to open the door,
Nor one of the Angels fair,
I'll expect you to greet me and welcome me in
When I make my entrance there.

— Rachel Titus

True leaders are not only content with the success of others, but are actually delighted to promote them and see them promoted. In my opinion it takes a great man to promote and release his wife and family. Let's reverse the phrase, "Behind every great man is a woman," and say, "Behind every great woman is a man who believes in her, supports her, and isn't resentful of the fact that she's a great leader." It's a mouthful to say, but it accurately describes the attitude that men should have when married to a woman leader.

Instead of you being the "bull in the china shop," be content to let your wife be the "china in the bull shop."

CHAPTER EIGHT
She says
life is always interesting

LIVING WITH A LEADER

DEVI Larry has described an aspect of various styles of leadership; namely the combination of his and my style and how we work together. Leadership is as varied as the people who fill the lead positions. Yet there are certain characteristics that all leadership shares.

My husband is a strong leader who has an introverted, melancholy temperament. He never seeks to be the life of the party, nor wastes time with trivial pursuits. He carefully plans his strategy to include personal relationships. He is comfortable with solitude and is companioned by meditation. He speaks seldom, but boldly, when he has something to say.

Now, I am a leader too, but one of a different kind, as Larry has clearly described. I like to be noticed when I enter a room, and solitude for any length of time, for me, is lonely. I speak about any subject as an expert, whether I know anything about it or not. Sometimes I really do know what I am talking about, and other times I will keep you guessing.

People are my life, sort of. Larry spends hours, days or months with one person at a time. His phone constantly rings with men from across the nation calling "Dad". But me? I like people in groups. So I create parties, dinner parties, birthday parties, going away parties or just parties. Who cares what they are for? Larry? He doesn't like parties, but he loves people. I think producing the party is the most enjoyable aspect of the party for me, not the party itself. I love to watch others enjoy something that I have created.

Though we are opposite in personality and approach, we still share common characteristics with all leaders. Understanding these distinctives makes living together a lot more pleasant.

Leaders have followers. Life with a leader always includes other people. His people and my people can be different. A common way for some to deal with a leader's "other" people is to become possessive and try to limit his or her relationships. Another is to isolate yourself and remain uninvolved and non-participatory in the leader's activities. Both of these options will hinder your relationship and should be rejected. Though you must schedule times to be alone with your spouse, the only true solution is to appreciate that your leader has others who are willing to follow. Enjoy participating, as much as possible, in the leadership area of his or her life.

Leaders have time demands. Schedules and deadlines are all part of the system a leader creates to reach his or her goals. Therefore, a spouse should seek to keep accurate calendars of dates and times, so he or she can approach each day with a feeling of preparedness, rather than chaos.

Communicate daily concerning your schedules and make adjustments for togetherness, whenever possible. Don't allow time demands to cause you to lead separate lives.

Leaders are focused. There is little room for spontaneity when living with a leader. Leaders are focused on their goals; schedules predetermine their activities. When you talk to focused people, you usually have only a portion of their attention. Their minds are always preoccupied and their attention span short, much like a child.

Don't take this personally. Rather, use several brief intervals of conversation, rather than pursuing a lengthy discussion. This way, you are more likely to keep your leader's interest.

Leaders work with staff. Leaders are accustomed to giving direction to a group of people working with them to implement their vision. They are in authority, and those on their team usually do not question that fact.

However, when leaders come home they often continue to treat family as staff. It helps to give a leader time for transition from the work environment to the family environment. Women, especially, must be careful about this. Your husband is not your personal assistant, your janitor, or your postman. Do not give him orders when you come home. You can help transition from a work mood to a home mood by creating a soft, warm ambiance—unlike the office—with music, candles, fragrance or other environmental props. Avoid noise and confusion.

Leaders carry stress. Leadership has stress points that are not always definable. Some things can be talked about but others are not quite so clear.

Pressures and concerns that cannot be talked about can alter his or her mood. Don't pile on more, but help carry the load.

Leaders can be wrong too. As my mother said, "What's so bad about being wrong?" Yet leaders feel such a responsibility to others, it is sometimes difficult for them to accept that they could be wrong. They may be concerned that their mistake could hurt those whom they are leading.

Therefore, leaders tend to want to cover their mistakes or justify them. Give your leader room to say, "I'm wrong," without fear of criticism. This attitude does wonders for providing the confidence to try again.

Leaders need affection. At home give one another lots of affection. Because your leader spouse spends their day with a team of people who support them, work with them, and interrelate in a close way, it is important that they connect with you when they come home. If you are distant and uninterested in them, it will be tempting for them to stay at work and become intimate with another person.

Living with a leader has challenges and rewards. The challenge is that you never know what is next. The reward is that life is always interesting.

About the authors
LARRY & DEVI TITUS

LARRY Larry Titus now devotes himself full-time to the mission of Kingdom Global Ministries, a non-profit organization he founded in 1992. The purpose of KGM is to relationally mentor, resource, and release the vision of global leaders.

Larry's thirty four years of senior pastoral leadership has developed congregations from small to large and from unhealthy to healthy. Because he comfortably crosses denominational and racial lines he has successfully established both inter-racial urban and suburban congregations. As a master communicator of the Word, Larry speaks to the "heart" of his audience.

The mentoring of men has been the strength of Larry's ministry. Many church leaders today were mentored by his discipleship. Authors have quoted him and men have followed him. Hundreds of prison inmates in Washington, California, Pennsylvania and even Europe have been influenced by his life and ministry. More than eighty men have lived in his home over his forty years of marriage and he is known as "Dad" by hundreds.

Larry has a 3M passion: Men, Ministers, and Missions. He impacts men's lives through retreats , conferences and the Men's Mentoring Intensives held at The Mentoring Mansion, a historical 8,000 square foot home that he and Devi use to mentor men and women in biblical responsibility. (Read more about The Mentoring Mansion under Devi Titus)

Larry's commitment to the Word, never wavering through deep trials, has produced fine churches, magazines, national and international ministries, but most importantly, a godly family. His wife Devi, and their adult children, Trina Titus Lozano and Dr. Aaron Titus are committed with him to live with integrity and to follow God's call wherever He leads.

About The Authors

DEVI   Devi Titus is among America's recognized Christian conference speakers and authors. She first came to the attention of women nationwide in 1978 when she founded and edited VIRTUE magazine, a successful Christian alternative to secular women's magazines. VIRTUE magazine for 22 years raised a standard of excellence for women's lives and for this work Devi Titus was presented the Superior Performance Award by the Washington Press Women Association.

Devi's life's passion is helping women to live in their full potential. In addition to conference speaking, she has now opened The Mentoring Mansion, an 8,000 square foot stunning historical home in Youngstown, Ohio where she trains women in a four-day Home Mentoring Intensive on creative home management and vital relationship skills. In addition, women are privileged to visit her personal home across the street and learn from her personal life. The Mentoring Mansion Ministry is committed to "restore the dignity and sanctity of the home by teaching women how to make their homes havens of rest and sanctuaries of love. In addition to the Home Mentoring Intensive, she has now begun a Haven Of Rest Intensive, teaching women on biblical meditation and anxiety free living.

Devi Titus is a leader of leaders. She serves on the advisory board for MINISTRIES TODAY magazine, and is on the Board Of Directors for the International Foursquare Gospel Church. She also serves on the board of Global Pastor's Wives Network.

Devi has partnered with her husband, Pastor Larry Titus, to establish five churches. They have two adult children, Trina Titus Lozano and Dr. Aaron P. Titus, and six grandchildren. However, she is a "mother" to many. Devi and her husband, Larry, have had over eighty young men and women live in their home over their forty years of marriage. Some were from prison or off the streets and others just coming to be mentored. "Follow me as I follow Christ—building the kingdom one person at a time" is the theme of their lives.

Whether Devi Titus writes or speaks as a pastor's wife, Bible teacher, publisher, mother, designer, editor, writer, speaker, homemaker or grandmother, she will motivate women and men to move towards fulfillment and godliness.

When you hear her speak, you do not forget what she says. As Bunny Wilson said, "You don't just meet Devi Titus, you experience her."

For more information contact:

Larry Titus
Kingdom Global Ministries
1848 Fifth Avenue
Youngstown, OH 44504
330-746-6780
www.kingdomglobal.com

Devi Titus
The Mentoring Mansion
1819 Fifth Avenue
Youngstown, OH 44504
330-746-6626
www.mentoringmansion.com

For additional resources:
www.livingsmart.org